P9-DEW-209

PRESCRIPTION OPIOIDS
AFFECTING LIVES

BY JEANNE MARIE FORD

MOMENTUM

Published by The Child's World®
1980 Lookout Drive • Mankato, MN 56003-1705
800-599-READ • www.childsworld.com

Photographs ©: Steve Heap/Shutterstock Images,
cover, 1; Red Line Editorial, 5; David Smart/
Shutterstock Images, 6; Fuss Sergey/Shutterstock
Images, 8; Alex Cambero Rodriguez/Shutterstock
Images, 10; SDI Productions/iStockphoto, 12;
Syda Productions/Shutterstock Images, 14; Iakov
Filimonov/Shutterstock Images, 16; Shutterstock
Images, 18, 20; Wave Break Media/Shutterstock
Images, 22, 28; SDI Productions/Shutterstock
Images, 24; Rowan Jordan/iStockphoto, 27

Copyright © 2021 by The Child's World®
All rights reserved. No part of this book may be
reproduced or utilized in any form or by any means
without written permission from the publisher.

ISBN 9781503844902 (Reinforced Library Binding)
ISBN 9781503846463 (Portable Document Format)
ISBN 9781503847651 (Online Multi-user eBook)
LCCN 2019957741

Printed in the United States of America

Some names and details have been changed
throughout this book to protect privacy.

CONTENTS

MOMENTUM

FAST FACTS

What It Is
► **Prescription** opioids are drugs prescribed by doctors to treat pain.

How They're Used
► These medications can be safe when used as prescribed.

► Misuse of prescription opioids involves using someone else's medication or using medication to get **high**.

► Risk of **addiction** increases if someone is on prescription opioids for more than three days.

Physical Effects
► Opioid use causes slowed breathing and an upset stomach.

► **Withdrawal** occurs when someone stops taking opioids. This causes vomiting, muscle pain, sweating, and anxiety.

► Opioid **overdose** can cause death.

Mental Effects
► Opioids block pain and make people who use them feel relaxed.

► Opioid use also causes confusion and tiredness.

Prescription Opioids and Heroin Use

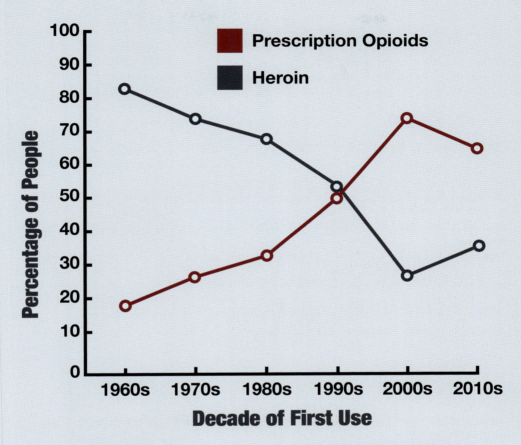

Cicero, T. J. et al. "The Changing Face of Heroin Use in the United States: A Retrospective Analysis of the Past 50 Years." *NCBI*, July 2014, ncbi.nlm.nih.gov. Accessed 20 Jan. 2020.

In the 1960s, more than 80 percent of people with heroin dependencies first used heroin rather than other opioids. By the early 2000s, that number decreased to about 30 percent. Instead, about 70 percent of people with heroin dependencies first used prescription opioids.

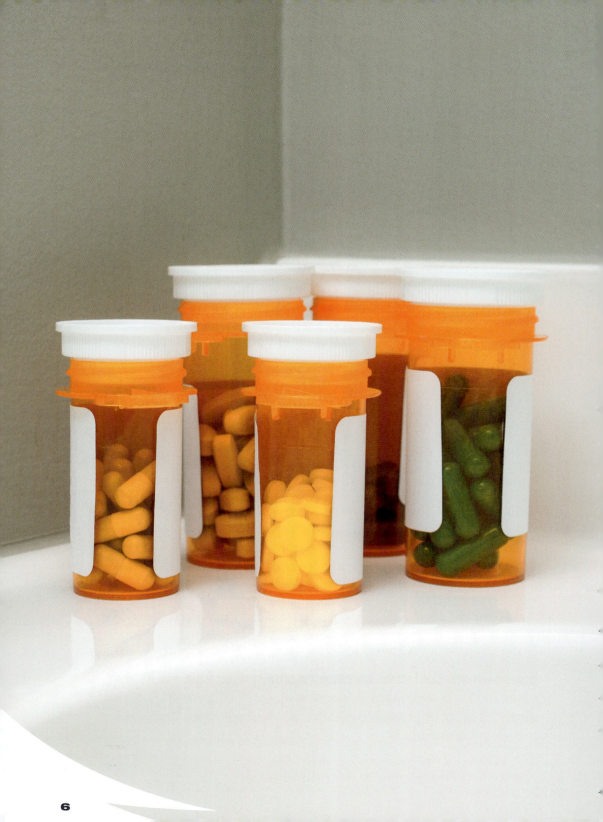

CHAPTER ONE

TAKING OPIOIDS ILLEGALLY

R yan shut the bathroom door behind him and locked it. He walked over to the medicine cabinet. When he opened it, he saw his mom's orange prescription bottle. Ryan read the instructions on how to use the pills on the bottle's white tag. His mom took a pill every few months for painful headaches. Ryan knew the medicine made her feel better. He'd been feeling depressed since his girlfriend broke up with him. He had also been cut from his high school's football team. Ryan picked up the bottle and screwed off the cap. He thought the pills might help him feel better, too.

It was easy to sneak the first pill without his mom noticing. Soon after he swallowed it, Ryan felt relaxed and happy. He liked the effect so much that he stole another pill the next day.

◄ **It is illegal for people to take pills a doctor prescribed to someone else.**

▲ **Drugs can cost a lot of money. Many people start stealing to pay for drugs.**

Within a few weeks, Ryan was **dependent** on opioids. He felt sick to his stomach every morning when he woke up. The sickness would only go away when he took another pill.

Ryan knew he couldn't keep stealing his mom's medicine. He didn't want her to find out he was using drugs. A friend at school introduced him to a dealer. If Ryan gave him money, the dealer got him more pills.

Ryan quickly realized drugs were expensive. He started using his lunch money to pay for the pills. He stole from his family. He broke into his little brother's piggy bank and blamed the housekeeper. Small lies turned into bigger ones. He hated the things he was doing, but not enough to stop. His body needed the drug. Now, he had to take four or five pills every day to stop himself from feeling sick. Ryan's body was adjusting to the drug use. Ryan needed more and more of the drug to get the same relaxed feeling.

At school, Ryan started hanging out with a new group of friends. They all used prescription drugs illegally, too. They partied together on weekends. One night, his friend Jeremy took too many pills. His face became pale, and he began sweating. His lips turned blue. Then, Jeremy fell to the ground.

Ryan heard his heart pounding in his ears. He raced to Jeremy's side and picked up his arm. It was limp. Ryan felt Jeremy's wrist for a pulse. He couldn't find it. Jeremy's heart wasn't beating, and he wasn't breathing.

Ryan knew Jeremy had overdosed on pills. Ryan screamed for his friends to call 911. He gave Jeremy CPR, pushing on his chest to keep him alive until an ambulance came. Most of Ryan's friends left before they found out if Jeremy would be okay. They were afraid of getting in trouble for using drugs illegally.

▲ **CPR can sometimes keep a person's heart beating until professional help arrives.**

Paramedics, people who respond to emergencies, arrived quickly. They told Ryan that Jeremy would have died if Ryan hadn't given him CPR.

A few weeks later, Ryan's phone lit up. He glanced at the bright screen and saw a text from a friend. Jeremy had overdosed again. This time, Jeremy had died. Ryan was scared. He knew there was a good chance he'd die if he didn't stop using drugs.

Ryan finally went to his mom and asked for help. She cried when he confessed that he was addicted to opioids. She took him to the doctor, who found a **rehabilitation** program that could help.

Ryan had to stay at the rehab home while he went through a drug **detox**. He was sick and miserable. He missed his home, his family, and his friends. But when he checked out 60 days later, he was finally drug-free. Ryan felt a lot more like his old self.

At home, his friends still used drugs. Dealers called his cell phone frequently. They wanted him to buy more pills so they could get money. Ryan was surrounded by temptation. He would have to fight every day for the rest of his life to resist using opioids.

GOOD SAMARITAN LAWS

The right thing to do when someone overdoses is to call 911. Sometimes friends and family members are afraid to call for help. They think they might get in trouble for using drugs illegally. Good Samaritan Laws typically protect people who call for help from being arrested. Samaritans are people who help others. States have different Good Samaritan Laws. These laws save lives.

CHAPTER TWO

PRESCRIPTION OPIOIDS TO HEROIN

When Randy reached down to dip his brush into a can of green paint, a bee flew in front of his face. He jerked away and lost his balance. His ladder swayed. Suddenly, he was falling. He felt a sharp pain in his foot as it hit the bottom step of the ladder on his way down.

At the hospital, the doctor told Randy he'd broken his heel. They sent him home with a cast, crutches, and a prescription for a powerful opioid painkiller. The pills took away the stabbing pain in Randy's foot. They also helped him relax and made his worries seem far away.

The doctor used a small electric saw to carefully cut off his cast several weeks later. The doctor told Randy the bone was healed. Randy was disappointed. He was hoping she would give him more opioid pills. He liked the way they made him feel.

◀ **Doctors prescribe a limited number of pills to help with pain.**

Getting drugs from somewhere other than pharmacies or a doctor is dangerous and illegal.

Randy claimed he still felt pain. The doctor didn't know Randy was lying. She wrote him another prescription.

When Randy ran out of pills a few weeks later, the doctor refused to give him more. She told Randy she didn't want him to become dependent on the medication. She didn't realize it was already too late.

Randy desperately wanted the feeling he'd gotten from his pain pills. He knew there was another drug out there that could give him the same kind of high. He found dealers on the street who would sell him heroin, an illegal opioid.

Randy became addicted to heroin after two weeks of using it repeatedly. It controlled his life and hurt his relationships.

He stole jewelry and cash to pay for drugs. One day, he was arrested for theft in front of his eight-year-old daughter, Meadow, and her friends. Meadow was humiliated. So was Randy.

After Randy got out of jail, he realized how quickly his drug use had gotten out of control. Randy was scared of wrecking his marriage and his relationship with his daughter. He decided to enter himself into a rehab program. Randy stayed in the program for 90 days. He felt a little more in control of his life when he returned home. His wife and Meadow welcomed him into the house with big smiles and hugs. They decided to make treats to celebrate. Randy's wife opened the cupboard and realized they were out of sugar to make cupcakes with. Randy volunteered to run to the grocery store.

He whistled happily as he walked down the street. Suddenly, he bumped into an old friend. Randy used to do heroin with her. Randy's friend asked him if he wanted to come back to her house. Randy knew she wanted to do drugs with him. He forgot all about the sugar and his family, who was waiting for him. He agreed to do heroin again.

After Randy used the heroin, he felt sick. He fell to his knees and couldn't breathe. He heard his friend ask if he was okay, but he couldn't respond. Randy's friend called an ambulance. Randy lost consciousness. When he woke up, he was in a hospital bed.

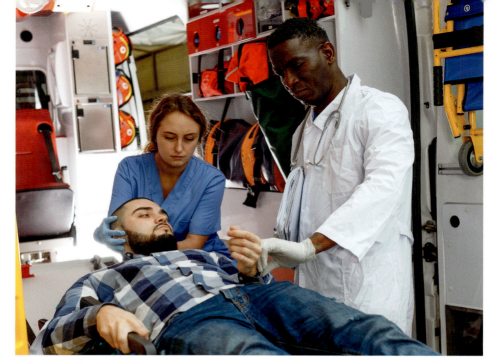

▲ **Paramedics may be able to save people from overdoses with Narcan.**

The doctor told Randy he had overdosed. Randy could have died if the paramedics hadn't saved him with a drug called Narcan. The Narcan reversed the effects of the heroin Randy had used.

Randy felt hopeless. He didn't think anything could help him with his addiction. Then, the doctor told Randy about a detox program. The doctor explained detox programs focused more on the physical effects of addiction, while rehab programs focused more on the mental effects. Randy doubted the detox program would work, but he would try anything to get better. He wanted to be the best husband and father he could be.

At the detox program, doctors gave Randy a medicine called Vivitrol. Vivitrol blocks the painkilling effect that opioids have. If someone tried taking opioids while on Vivitrol, he wouldn't experience any of their effects. In the program, Randy was able to stop focusing on how much he wanted opioids. Instead, he focused on how much he wanted to be with his family.

The doctors gave Randy a shot of Vivitrol once a month for 16 months. Randy was able to live his life without constantly thinking about opioids. Meadow made him promise he would work hard on his recovery. Randy had broken many promises to his daughter over the years, but this one he planned to keep.

TREATING AN OVERDOSE

Naloxone is a drug that can reverse the effects of an opioid overdose. It also helps people breathe. Naloxone is available as either a nasal spray, known as Narcan, or an injection. Many police officers and paramedics use Naloxone to treat patients they suspect have had opioid overdoses. More than one dose of Naloxone may be needed.

CHAPTER THREE

IMPACT ON FAMILIES

Tyler raced down the green field toward the goal. He dribbled the soccer ball and weaved between opposing players. Then, he took aim and kicked the ball to the right side of the net. The goalie reached toward the ball but couldn't stop it in time. Tyler's face broke into a large smile. He had scored his first goal!

Parents on the sidelines cheered. Tyler was 11 years old and had just started playing for a new soccer team. He looked toward the sidelines, hoping to see his mom's happy face. But she hadn't shown up to his game. Tyler felt his heart sink.

He was distracted for the rest of the game. His mom had promised that she would be there. But for the past few months, Tyler's mom hadn't been acting like herself. One minute she would be smiling, and the next she would start yelling. It was hard for Tyler to guess how his mom would react to small things.

◄ **Parents with addictions may miss important events, such as sports games, in their child's life.**

▲ **People are sometimes prescribed opioids for back pain and other injuries.**

His mom also slept a lot, and she wasn't interested in Tyler's life anymore.

During halftime, Tyler stood apart from his teammates. He was so sad that he almost felt sick. Tyler missed how his mom used to drive him to and from soccer practice and games.

Now he usually got a ride with his teammate Ryan. Tyler's mom also stopped volunteering at his school. They used to laugh and have fun together. But things had changed since her back injury six months ago. She had been in horrible pain. The pain had gotten so bad that her doctor had prescribed her opioids to help.

Ever since then, Tyler had seen his mom taking more and more of her prescription opioid pills. He knew she was taking too many, because she lied and told Tyler she was taking less. Once, he heard his mom talking on the phone with her doctor. She claimed that she had lost her prescription, and needed another one to help with her back pain. But Tyler knew that wasn't true. He had seen the empty orange pill bottle in the trash. His mom had already taken all the medication and needed even more.

After the soccer game, Tyler slowly walked to the parking lot. He watched as his teammates and their parents packed into their cars and drove off. Tyler bit his bottom lip and tried not to cry. He didn't have a ride home. He had told Ryan his mom would drive him, but she never showed up. As Tyler started to panic, his coach came up to him and asked where Tyler's mom was.

Since his mom's addiction had started, Tyler hadn't told anyone about it. His dad wasn't around, and he didn't want to scare his grandparents. But the concern in his coach's eyes made Tyler feel like he could share. Tyler told his coach everything.

▲ **People find support in peers and counselors at rehab.**

His coach listened. Then, his coach suggested that they call Tyler's grandparents. The four of them met for a late lunch, and Tyler told his grandparents what had been going on at home. He realized that his grandparents shared his concern. They had noticed changes in their daughter's behavior, but they hadn't realized what was happening.

Tyler felt as though a huge weight had been lifted off his chest. He was still worried about his mom, but he felt less alone now. His grandparents came up with a plan to help Tyler's mother.

The three of them went to talk with Tyler's mom. They each told her how worried they were about her.

When his mom started crying, Tyler was surprised. His mom said that she knew she needed help, but couldn't stop taking the prescription opioids on her own. Tyler's mom was willing to stop using drugs, and she agreed to go to rehab. There, she would be **sober** and could learn how to handle her addiction. Meanwhile, Tyler could live with his grandparents.

The day Tyler's mom went to rehab, she pulled him into a tight hug. She promised that she would try her hardest to stay sober. Tyler had a feeling they would have a long road ahead of them, but he was hopeful that he would get his mom back one day.

TREATING OPIOID ADDICTION

Rehab facilities help people recover from opioid dependency and addiction. One of the phases of rehab is detox. Medications can lessen the impact of withdrawal and help patients stay in treatment. Along with taking medication, people can attend family therapy and behavioral counseling. Behavioral counseling helps people change their habits. Treatment and counseling continue after the rehab program ends. Fighting addiction is a lifelong battle.

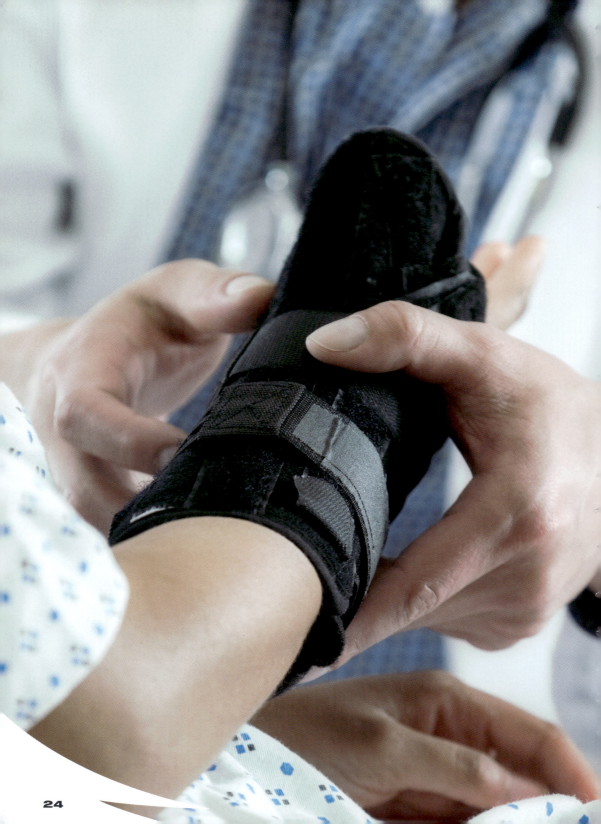

CHAPTER FOUR

A DOCTOR'S ADDICTION

Kathy balanced a box of brightly colored goodie bags as she crossed the parking lot. Her son, the birthday boy, waved from the playground as he sped down the twisty slide. Kathy didn't see the curb beneath her until she tripped. Goodie bags flew in every direction, spilling toy cars onto the pavement. Kathy broke her fall with her hand. She heard a sickening popping sound.

Kathy was a doctor, and she immediately knew her wrist was badly broken. At the hospital, she had surgery to pin the bones back together. When Kathy woke up, she was in terrible pain. She took a prescription opioid every three to four hours to help ease the pain, just as her doctor directed.

When she got home, Kathy was frustrated that she couldn't do normal household work or do fun things with her broken wrist.

◄ **People who take painkillers for an injury may get addicted to them.**

One day, she had a fight with her husband about household chores. She felt like crying afterward. When she took her pain pill, it was easier to ignore her troubles. But the pain pills only made her feel relaxed for a short while.

Kathy didn't take all the pills from her prescription. She saved a few to take when she felt stressed at work or home. At her job, she was surrounded by **narcotics**. One day when she had a very bad headache, she injected herself with a patient's leftover opioid painkiller. The feeling of calmness was instant and powerful. She knew she was doing something very wrong and promised herself she wouldn't do it again. But the next day, her headache returned, and she injected more medicine.

After three months, Kathy was taking ten times the dose of narcotics she'd used the first time. She passed out in the hospital bathroom after injecting drugs. When she woke up, she realized she'd thrown up all over herself. She cleaned up the vomit, changed her clothes, and went back to work.

A few weeks later, her bosses questioned Kathy about the drugs that were disappearing during her work shifts. She was finally forced to admit she had a problem. Even her husband was shocked. Kathy didn't drink or smoke. She was the last person he would have expected to develop an addiction to drugs.

**Hospitals keep different kinds of ►
prescription drugs in stock.**

▲ **Along with rehab, meditation can help people battle the stress of addiction.**

Kathy attended a drug rehab program for five months. She went to therapy sessions during the day and came home at night. She was busy, but it was worth it. After she completed the program, she continued to attend meetings with a sponsor.

Sponsors help people keep their goals of making healthier decisions. Kathy also used meditation and yoga to keep her recovery on track. Meditation may include sitting still or exercising. It helps people clear their minds and become calm.

After two years in recovery, Kathy was allowed to begin practicing medicine again. She was closely supervised for the first few months. Being surrounded by opioid medication every day was a constant temptation she had to fight.

Rather than being ashamed and hiding her history of addiction, Kathy shared her story often. She wanted to spread awareness that drug addiction could happen to anyone.

THINK ABOUT IT

► What would you do if a friend or family member was misusing prescription opioids?
► What can doctors do to try to reduce the risks of opioid misuse?
► Drug addiction can ruin relationships. Why do you think some people keep using drugs even when they are hurting the people they love?

INDEX

ABOUT THE AUTHOR

Jeanne Marie Ford is an Emmy-winning TV scriptwriter who holds a Master of Fine Arts degree in writing for children from Vermont College. She has written numerous children's books and articles. Ford also teaches college English. She lives in Maryland with her husband and two children.